6.95

Jim Metcalf's Journal

Jim Metcalf's Journal

by Jim Metcalf

Photographs by Ken Youngblood

PELICAN PUBLISHING COMPANY
Gretna 1976

Manufactured in the United States of America

Published by Pelican Publishing Company, Inc.
630 Burmaster Street, Gretna, Louisiana 70053

Designed by Dwight Agner

1st printing: October, 1974
2nd printing: August, 1976

Contents

The Poet and the Flowers   9
Togetherness   11
Obsession   13
Flirtation   15
Love   17
The Republic   19
Class Reunion   21
New Orleans   23
The Time Between   25
The Prisoner   27
Wanderer   29
Seasons   31
Reincarnation   33
The Children   34
Interim Manifesto   35
For Not So Young Lovers   37
Secrets   38
Windows   41
Lifestyle   43
Requiem for a Leaf   45
Sea   46
The Day the Toys Died   49
Parenthood   51
Auto Junkyard   53
Art   54
A Farewell to Dreams   56
Judgment Day   58
Crossroad   59
Bourbon Street at Dusk   63

Jim Metcalf's Journal

The Poet and the Flowers

Once again we are betrayed,
the words and I . . .
faced with a challenge we cannot meet.
We cannot translate the quiet splendor
of a flower
into symbols set on paper . . .
or sounds the symbols signify.

We are impotent,
the words and I.
Inept, incapable,
awkward jesters of the court
mumbling through the sacred halls
        of beauty's majesty.

How could we presume
to describe the sweetness of a rose?
Colors heightened by the dew upon it,
        tears of happiness
shed upon its petals
when heaven saw the wonder
        it had made.

We admit defeat,
the words and I.
We cannot tell the story
of the flowers.
They do not need our counsel.
They have counsel with the angels.

Yet, if the last wondrous
bud should die,
and there would never be another
to replace it.
The angels would be as weak as we.
They could not find words to say farewell,
or music to sing a hymn
            in parting.
The angels could not say goodbye.
The angels would be weeping.

Togetherness

We walk where thousands walk
    among a sea of faces.
We hear the footsteps of those
who share with us
this time and place.
Yet, we walk alone and
    we are afraid.
For we cannot know what lives
behind the eyes that are reluctant
    to meet other eyes
in this gathering of strangers.
    We do not ask.
    We do not care.
Content we are to be left alone
in the throng.
To be passed by as we are passing . . .
unhurt, untouched,
save perhaps, the brushing of a shoulder
as we go our separate ways.
    Sing!
       A song of kindred souls.
    Hail!
       The brotherhood of man.

Obsession

If I am obsessed,
then let my affliction be
     a lust for beauty.
And let my search for it
     be in all places
and at all times.
And let it be
     never ending.

Help me to find it
where others have looked
and seen only ugliness.

In fields of weeds
     where wild winds
blow the vagrant sand,
show me some hidden desert flower,
     rich and full blooming . . .

A sprig of grass beneath
     the city's muddy snow
when Spring waits for the end
     of a malingering Winter.

Let me know
        the touch
of tiny hands . . .
        the scent
of summer mornings before the sun . . .
        the sounds
of laughter and muted organs
where stained glass windows are . . .
        the taste
of berries from vines
that cling to country fences.

And when the search leads me
to places that are barren,
        where no beauty is,
help me to create it.
To leave some sign
that there was one who passed
        and cared.

Flirtation

There was a time
when I could read the looks
on maidens' faces.
When I was young with roving heart,
I could see the faintest traces
of invitation
that flashed in eyes
that met my eyes.
And I could recognize
flirtation.

And I knew just what to do
to perpetuate the moment.
Knew how to smile
and be blasé.
Knew what putting on a show meant.

But somewhere between those days
and now,
I've lost my power to interpret.
And when I see a stray glance
come my way from some young
passing beauty,
I am frozen in dismay,
not knowing if I should look back ...
Not knowing what to say ...
without the slightest hint
of the intent
Behind the look she gives me.

Could be she finds the gray
that streaks my hair, suggests
worldly wisdom and maturity . . .
irresistible sophistication
and experienced impurity.

But I fear there is another possibility
and its consideration makes me sad.
Could be she looks at me that way
because I remind her of her dad.

Love

Of all the words in the language . . . "love" is, beyond a doubt, the most overworked, misused, most inclusive, talked about, written about, and perhaps most misunderstood. Ordinarily, the first thing that comes to mind when the word is mentioned is that ecstatic and mysterious relationship between boy and girl.

It can come, they say, at first sight or it can come slowly, as the two grow to know each other and decide they must be in love because they'd rather be together than apart. And sometimes they are right, it is indeed love. But as they grow older, they will find that the word means a lot of other things too—in fact, most things that are really worthwhile. They will find it is made up more of giving than of getting, more of helping than being helped, more of listening than of talking, more of seeing than being seen.

And they will find there is no such thing as loving a little bit; that it is pure and cannot be diluted, that it is total and only the *total* can be increased, strengthened, and broadened as their capacity to love increases. And whatever that capacity, it must be full at all stages of its development. And they will find it everywhere, this overworked word. In quiet places where the sun that streams through stained glass windows lights the faces of people, heads bowed in prayer. In hands that reach out to help and grasp a weaker hand, saying what no words can say. In eyes that sparkle still from wrinkled faces when friendly footsteps pad across antiseptic floors toward a bed that death is watching. In the voices of children as they clutch some tiny bit of fur that strayed from some unwanted litter, and the words, "Can I keep him please? I'll care for him . . . and I've already given him a name."

And they will find love in solitude. Sometime when the

world is far away and nature's wonders are all about, there'll be a sudden warmth and at the long day's dying they'll know they're not alone at all and that they will never be.

The Republic

Consider now, man's noble dream of freedom . . . this Republic . . . this America. If it should die suddenly one day, one day without the sounds of battle to signal its dying, if it were to slip away quietly in the sleep of our indifference, who would be the messengers of its defeat? And how would they tell the tale of a fallen colossus, and how it died, and why?

Would they say the dreams of those who gave it life were foolish and impractical? That those whose hands, in classic script, put ink to paper and fashioned words more fitting for the poet to ponder than for a nation to build its laws upon? Would they say young men of over half a dozen generations died for naught because they held those words near sacred? Or would they see that, imperfect though it was, it was not the framework that killed the nation . . . rather, it was the people; their apathy, their indifference, their taking it all for granted, like most things that were theirs, and assuming it would be forever . . . shaking their heads and shrugging when some symptom of an illness came to light and cried that it needed healing. The people, demanding with constant vigor the rights they were guaranteed, yet unwilling to claim responsibility for the ills that threatened that guarantee.

And perhaps, they would mention greed, these messengers of defeat. The greed of those in high places who would sell it all for a price, and the greed of the common man who demands his due while denying that of his neighbor.

It's a child, in years, as compared to other nations. A youth that leads the world. It is for us to nurture it, and not the other way. And if it should die of our neglect, the blood of the freedom that gave it life will stain our hands, and the clanging of the chains of bondage will echo from the mountain tops and through the desolate valleys of a barren land.

Class Reunion

The last paragraph of the letter read:

"And so Jim, we of the High School Homecoming Celebration Committee sincerely hope you can be with us and all your old classmates next month. As you know, this will be the first time we have ever attempted to get our graduating class together. It has been a long time since those wonderful pre-war years and we will, I am sure, have much to talk about."

Regards,
Dick Martin, Chairman

Dear Dick,

I regret that I will not be able to be with you for the homecoming celebration. I must be frank and tell you that it is neither the press of business nor the lack of time that precludes my being there. Rather it is fear. Fear that something very precious to me might be destroyed . . . the memories of those days, filled with the magnificent bewilderment of youth, when we were lean and eager, absurdly naive, summertime free and hopelessly in love with living.

I like to pretend that the people and the places are still there, just as they were when last I saw them. And sometimes, when it's important that I remember what being young was like, I go back in memory to those days.

If I were to see them now, the people and the places and the changes time has brought, my little game of make-believe would be over. It would fade into the world of reality that is, I believe, too much with us. There would be middle-aged people where children were supposed to be, fat where once there was muscle, and wrinkles would replace the dimples I recall on certain freckled faces.

And the places . . . the vacant lots . . . the gridirons of chilly Saturday afternoons in autumn, baseball diamonds under July's burning sun; they would not be vacant now, for progress would have grown in places that had felt the footsteps of our youth. And there would be plastic booths where tables with wrought iron legs and marble tops once held the sweet and wondrous delicacies from the soda fountain at Old Man Peters' drug store . . . and it would be air-conditioned. Gone would be the drone of wooden overhead fans that mingled with the talk of English Four, and who was going steady.

So if you will, Dick, give my regrets and tell all I'll be thinking of them. And when you hear them tell each other how they've changed, tell them that to me . . . they haven't . . . . . .

Sincerely,
Jim

New Orleans

I turn away for just a little while,
then look back and you've grown some more.
The stone and steel of your towers
rising above your river
hold back the sunlight from the streets below.
Streets that wind and stretch and reach outward
to unintended places.
Through the swampland . . . into the forests and beyond.
And the sounds of the city are heard
where only yesterday silence was.
What are the dimensions of this dream you follow?
How far will your cold and windowed columns
penetrate the sky?
What star to grasp?
What mountain top to gaze down upon?
And this web of asphalt and cement you weave . . .
these roads . . . these highways with obscure patterns
like cracked glaze on cheap dishes,
Where will they end?
What is their outer limit?
Follow your dream if you must.
But don't be obsessed with size
and growth.
Nor misled by the misconception
that giants are always strong.
Don't get too big, too soon.
And above all,
never forget what you really are . . .
this beautiful old enchantress . . .
this siren at the bend of the river . . .
this New Orleans.

The Time Between

I cannot recall when first I came to know
I was no longer young.
Suddenly, I was walking in the twilight
that glows between the years
of youth and those when we are old.
And now I find this wondrous world of
in between
holds the better parts of both.

I see loveliness and beauty
I had not the time to see before,
when youth's desires,
immediate and demanding,
blinded me to everything,
save the fever of the moment.

This twilight is the perfect time.
Would that I could hold it always.
But I fear that someday soon,
perhaps as I lay sleeping
in the darkness of these fleeting days,
my years will come upon me.
And when I awake
I will be old
and with uncertain hands that tremble,
I will grasp a cane to lean upon.

And I will see the beauty
that surrounds me now
through faded eyes.
And the colors of the sky
and all that lies beneath it
will be faded too.

So I will drink deeply of life's wine
while there is time to taste it.
And I will drink as much as I can hold.
And when it's over,
I will turn down
      an empty glass.

The Prisoner

My soul could write a million poems
if it were but free.
Compose a million symphonies . . .
Paint canvases to line the walls
of all the galleries in the world . . .
If it were but free.
But it is not.
It is the slave of me.
And though it begs to be released
and create its wondrous things,
I am an unrelenting master.
I draw the drapes of ugliness
That hold back the light
from the windows of my soul.
I let the chains of adverse circumstance
lock the doorways that lead to freedom.
And when the vagrant winds of discontent
blow chill within me
I resent the capability
of my prisoner.
And wish that it were strong enough
to break its bonds—
to free itself—
and make of me the slave.

Wanderer

I do not know what voice it is that calls to me
and beckons me to follow.
I do not know whence it comes, or why.
I know only that it makes within me
a restlessness
that compels me to go on searching,
as I have searched through all my years.

I have followed trails of steel
that cross the meadows and the marshes
and the mountains.
And I have seen the faces of those
along the way,
peering through doors
half open . . .
through windows
without curtains.

I have roamed the silent, tranquil skies
close to where the stars are.
I have outrun sunsets.
I have looked down
on eagles flying.
And watched the carefree, cotton clouds
meet with others of their kind,
convene, turn darker and then conspire
to mold a tempest,
and frighten lovers,
playing in the sun.

With swollen sails above my head
I have bowed to the will
of wayward winds
and touched the face of oceans.

I have found uncharted, secret isles
that no one knows but me.
And I have walked alone
along their shores.

But the voice that calls
and echoes through my days and nights
eludes me still.
And I must go on searching.
I have not the time to rest.

Seasons

The seasons are my undoing.
They make of me a fickle lover.
I see Autumn's face
in every face I see.
And I am overcome.
I cannot recall the look of Spring
that held my fancy
in the soft kiss of a quiet rain
last April.
All that was put aside
when first I felt the sweet, fresh
breath of Fall,
my latest love,
yet, most likely, not my last.
For it is the way of vagrant hearts
to trade one enchantment for another;
to hold one for a little while
before the search begins
for one that will replace it.
But for now, I will let Autumn's
charms caress me,
Before December's snows will part us.
Then I'll forget her face
as I forgot the face of April
when first I felt October's kiss.

Reincarnation

I do not want to live again
without the loves that I have known.
I do not want my soul
to be given to another
when my breath is stilled.
For whatever life might lie ahead
could not be half as wondrous
as the one I left behind.

For I have known the truths
that life is made of.
Known love,
have given and received it.
Known beauty,
and seen the face of God
reflected in it.

What more could I
look forward to?

They say I would not recall
that there was another time.
I do not believe it.
I think that, somehow,
I would always hear the songs
        of other violins
and smell the sweetness
        of other roses.

The Children

These fleeting moments
of your sunshine years,
these warm and golden seconds of your nights and days,
too soon will pass . . .
And leave you with half remembered moments
with no sequence.
Each a fading entity unto itself . . .
unrelated to any other.
Like shadows they will come and go;
the Christmas lights . . .
the birthday cakes . . .
the red balloons . . .
The brand new bikes
and popcorn from a paper bag
that dad held in the park one day.
Was it Spring?
Or was it Summer?
You will not recall
except that it was warm and nice
and that he laughed
and rode you on his shoulders.

If you could hold just one day of now
and remember it forever,
through all your dawns and dusks
and seasons giving way to seasons,
there would always be a part of you
the years could never change.
And though you might have seen
a hundred winters
there would be a certain look
of April in your eyes.

Interim Manifesto
(after graduation—before marriage)

>This life I hold;
>this life that is me,
>is mine.
>And I alone will live it.
>
>Its patterns will be of my design.
>Mine too, the dreams
>that give it meaning.
>And its loves
>and hates
>and all its other fevers.
>
>This life is mine
>to keep
>or put aside.
>The choice is mine.
>And I alone will do the choosing.

For Not So Young Lovers

Youth has ended,
tomorrow we will be old.
Walk with me today
in the fading hours of this beautiful
in-between.
Hold my hand
and together we will go where we've never been
nor will e'er be again.
We will not dwell on what is gone
when youth's fever brought us each to each.
Nor on tomorrow's chilling winds of age.
We will set aside this day
to stand alone, independent of what has been
or will be.
Answerable not to calendars,
or clocks, or suns or moons
or tides that toll the knell of time.
And if it should be reported
sometime generations hence,
that a day is missing
from the charts men use to count the days,
we'll smile from some corner of eternity
and confess.
We took it, it was ours,
that day when spring was all about
and April begged to come inside.
We took it.
You can never have it back again.

Secrets

I do not ask why,
when suddenly in your eyes
I see a certain look
that does not fit the setting we are in,
the place, the pattern of our conversation.
A haunting look, and soft and wistful.

I do not ask what brought it there.
Or what it means.
But I know it is not of my doing.
And I am no part of it.

I know you must be hearing music
I have not heard.
Or words, perhaps,
whispered in another place.
Or remembering a springtime dream that died
when summer ended.

I wonder but I do not ask.
Because to love is not to own.
And we love because of what we know,
one about the other.
And that is all we need;
All that is important.

There is a special, secret place
where part of us is kept.
We save tiny remnants
from the fabric of our lives
and store them there.
And they are not for sharing.
Not to be judged
for their merit
or their logic.
Not to be passed upon . . .
save by the keeper of the keys
who alone can open the door
to the place wherein they dwell . . .
save by the one who put them there.

So I will not ask why,
when I lose you for a moment;
when I see that look upon your face.

And I will not answer
if you should ask
when you see it
on mine.

Windows

The stories windows tell are told in silence.
Like pages from a book when you're alone.
No sound is needed to tell the tale.
Windows that, like picture frames, enclose
tiny segments of lives
and hold them for a second before the scene
changes to some other.
Some tell of warmth and love and happiness
that dwell on the other side.
The side no passerby can see.
Save for a fleeting moment before the drawing
of the drapes shuts out the light
that overcomes the sudden darkness of a winter evening.
There are stories of violence the windows tell.
Boarded now, they tell of tragedy
and of how suddenly it came.
And how unexpectedly.
And how it touched the lives
of all who knew.
There are stories of despair they tell.
The windows whose dirty glass
reflects the hopelessness of poverty
where tired feet in worn-out shoes
shuffle down streets filled with the rubbish
that remains after hope has gone.
And there are windows that tell of man's desire
to own that which he cannot afford to buy.
See them as they beckon and entice
and show the stuff a sparkling dream
is made of.

Are they true
these stories that the windows tell
or are they sometimes make-believe?
You'll never really know for sure,
unless you see them from the other side.

Lifestyle

I am less afraid of dying
than of living without my loves;
the nearness of my dear, sweet people;
the music of words that sing to me
and the words that music speaks;
and colors
and sweet smelling things;
the touch of certain hands
and the changing moods of skies
when seasons change;
the magnificent arrogance of roses;
the majesty of eagles flying.

If I should be left with none of these,
then death would be my consolation.
And if darkness should be
the end of all of it,
what difference would there be?
To trade one world of darkness for another?
More to be feared than dying
is having love and beauty all around
And being part of neither.

Requiem for a Leaf

The covenants of spring have been fulfilled.
The promises of April kept.
You have lived your promised days.
And now, in beauty you are dying.

You have known the warmth of friendly suns ...
The sweet, soft kiss of rains in summer ...
danced on the wings of sudden breezes
to the music of feathered minstrels.
Felt the nearness of clouds above your head
and heard whispers from the lips of lovers
in shadows, sun flecked, at your feet.

And suddenly, it's over.
And it was all so fast.
Yet, you have known of life
all that is worthwhile to know.
Known beauty, all that is important.

So now, in the rich and splendid colors
of the robe of death you wear,
release your grasp and go
in loveliness.

Cling not to what is gone.
For the splendor that adorns you now
will fade.
And leave a shrunken, ugly thing
waiting for a spring that will not come;
denying death its pledge of beauty
with your passing.

Sea

I have walked in silence along your shores.
Have watched the changing patterns
of your moods.
And heard the songs you sing
to accompany them.

In the still of midnights,
summer warm and star laden
I have seen you.
Seen your face move gently in the
slow and certain cadence
of the breath of sleep.

Then, after waking,
in drowsy half awareness,
toy with a reflection of the moon
and change its shape
like the distorted mirror in a fun house
where we used to go
on summer holidays.

I have heard the sounds your ships make
crawling through a fog that covers you.
Heard their whistles
and their bells
and the voices of their men
cursing their maker for their blindness;
praying to their maker for deliverance.

I have seen you in sudden summer rages,
gray with anger;
frothing and screaming
and ravaging the land
and all upon it.
Taking that to which you have
no rightful claim.

Then, as if remorseful,
I have seen you give freely
of your treasures.
Seen you fill the holds of fishing ships.
Seen the life's blood of a nation
taken from your depths;
transfused by the towers of steel
that rise above you.

And I have heard your music
when you caress the sandy beaches
of a certain, far off place . . .
A secret island place
that no one knows,
but you and me.

The Day the Toys Died

It had been raining most of the long afternoon and she had been staring out the window at the gray shrouded landscape for easily an hour. The soft light from the lamp was reflected like a new and shiny penny in the copper colored halo that was her hair.

In her eyes there was a certain sadness I had never seen before. And there was hurt there . . . and confusion. She was lost in the subtle and bewildering twilight that separates the fantasies of babyhood and the realities of adolescence. She was filling a cardboard box with toys that only yesterday had been so very real; so splendidly talented with versatility enough to play any role in the theatre of make-believe.

But, overnight, it seemed they had lost their powers and had become mere reminders of another time; a time that would never be again. She would, she said, give them to some *little* girl, now that she'd outgrown them.

She had packed them all away, save for a strange and faded little creature. We never knew just what it was. Some said it was a rabbit; others a kangaroo . . . a bear. But it really didn't matter. It was the object of her deepest love and together they had supped and slept. And walked and talked, and there was seldom one without the other.

She held it at arms length now, looking squarely into its face. Then suddenly she pulled it close to her, the way she used to when she was lonely or in trouble. She whispered something. I could not hear what. I was not supposed to. Then in sudden sweeping motion, she put it in the box and closed the flap and quietly left the room. She made no sound when she passed by me, but I could feel her crying.

And now she knew much of what life is made of. That there cannot be love without pain and the things we love are merely borrowed. And that one day, in one way or another, we will lose them.

And now she was aware that there cannot be growth without sacrifice and that there is no guarantee that what will come tomorrow will be half as precious as what was ours just yesterday.

Parenthood

The main trouble with being a parent is that you can't learn how to be one until you already are . . . if, in fact, you can learn at all.

There is a certain amount of preparation that can be done beforehand . . . you can read a lot about parenthood . . . you can talk with people who are parents . . . but that's sort of like reading a book on flying and talking with a pilot, then jumping into a plane all alone and taking off.

And besides, the baby hasn't read the recommended literature or talked the situation over with anybody, so he's going to play the game as he sees it . . . ad lib all the way.

And if you have more than one, you have no doubt found that what worked for one will not necessarily work for another . . . . So what it boils down to is that you are one parent . . . or three . . . or four . . . depending on the number of children you have . . . one likes peanut butter . . . another prefers cold chili. It's hard to set down guidelines that all your progeny will even understand . . . much less follow.

And there is a point where the whole thing becomes academic. A point where they're not listening to anything you say anyway.

And it's then you realize you have raised a child . . . that your tutoring years are over, as far as he's concerned.

Now it's just a matter of hoping and waiting to see how it all turns out.

And if you see that you've made a mistake or two along the way, you might be given a second chance and you can tell your children how to raise their children . . . but don't bet your social security check they'll be listening . . . .

Auto Junkyard

Behold the cadavers left behind
by a civilization on the move.
Rusting relics that tell of
the restlessness of man.
Of how he runs and how motion
is more important than direction.

And when that which had propelled him
in his flight, failed
somewhere along the way,
when there was no life left in it,
he paused only long enough
to grab another painted carriage
on the passing carrousel
and set out on his way again.

And on his journey,
He will pass the same point many times.
And the beginnings
And the endings
will become as one.
A melding of infinities.

And these skeletons of steel
he leaves behind,
these hulls he brands as worthless
because they no longer move,
have a destiny fairer than his own.
For they will be reshaped . . . remolded
and made to live again.
What man can be certain
that he will?

Art

To leave behind some vestige of the thoughts we had . . .
the things we felt . . .
Some tangible evidence that proclaims us to be
more than things
that walked and breathed
and for a time occupied some tiny space
in this universe.
This is the dream eternal of those who would create.
Those who would leave something of themselves . . .
something not here
before their coming.
A creation like no other . . .
as no man is like another.
And if it be beautiful to behold,
many will be the happier for it.
And if it is judged to be otherwise . . .
So be it.
If, in honesty it reflects
a thought . . .
a mood
or transient fantasy
of its creator,
art's purpose has been served.
The artist has had his say.
And perhaps, on some tomorrow
with changing circumstance,
there will be one to gaze upon it
and see beauty there.
Some someone
who understands.

Canvas, hung in half forgotten places . . .
Metal made red with heat
and molded . . .
Metal now grown cold . . .
Words that fade
on yellow, brittle paper . . .
These things and ten thousand others
say,
"I have lived.
I have felt.
And this I leave
as part of both."

A Farewell to Dreams

You can look back on them now and smile,
those dreams you vowed one day to own.
There were so many of them
and so few really worth the wanting.
Can you remember even half of them?
Or did they die and fade from mind
when a closer look killed the desire
that burned when seen from far away?

And the ones that did survive;
the dreams that stayed alive
through all the years
yet, were never to be fulfilled;
what of them, now that it's too late
to ever grasp them?

They will die.
They must.
But it's pointless to mourn their passing.
Think not so much of them,
as of all the good that came your way
without your even asking.
Perhaps these were the dreams of another,
of one who worked, yet saw them die.
They went to you instead
without your even trying.

Dwell not on what might have been
but on what has.
Be grateful for the road you've walked.
Forget the one not taken.

Judgment Day
(Circa 1900)

Withered Sunday afternoon ladies
after church,
around a quilting frame,
drinking milk
and eating cookies
and talking about Jesus
and Canaan land
and Jennifer Drummer.
            She's pregnant.
Could see it plain as day,
in church this morning,
underneath her choir robe
when she stood up straight.
She's showing, right enough and
            she's just fourteen.
            Just a child.
God'll punish her for sure.
A *sinful* child.
            And him too,
            whoever he is.
The Lord hates fornicators,
children or not.
Let us pray ...
Lord, bless this food
and this drink
            to the nourishment
            of our bodies.
                  Amen!
                        Amen.

Crossroad

A parent to one who is no longer a child
and is leaving home for the first time

Soon now this path we've walked together . . .
the only one you've ever known,
will become two roads.
I will take the shorter one
that ends somewhere around a sudden turn
not far from here.
You will take the longer of the two.
The one that leads as far as you can see . . .
and beyond.
The one we all walk down alone
when life is young
and time is of no great consequence.
The road's the same for all of us.
But what we do along the way . . .
the byways we choose to take
or pass on by . . .
The stops we make
to consider some elusive, beckoning goal . . .
And those we meet
and choose to walk beside
and share what lies ahead . . .
These things make each journey
unlike any other.
And how do we part
now that the fork of the road
is in full view?
Do we say goodbye
and try to smile?
Then turn our backs
and walk away?

Then look back and wave
and take one final turn
and wait to hear the footsteps of the other
grow fainter ...
And finally die away?
No ... we will not do that at all.

You will take your road.
And you will walk away ...
And look ahead ...
And think ahead.
And I'll be here at the crossroads
until you disappear
over the horizon.
Then I'll take mine.
And it won't take long to reach the end,
so I'll walk ever so slowly.
And should you find
the meadows that line your way
less green than those you knew before ...
Come back ...
Call for me.
And I'll be close enough to hear.
And we will save the parting
for another day.

Bourbon Street at Dusk

Time to get up now, you tired old sinner.
You've been resting all day
behind those drapes you closed this morning,
just as the sun was coming up
and the day people were beginning to stir.

They're turning on your lights now,
so it's time to roll out . . .
cake on the make-up
and put those sparkling things in your hair . . .
those glittery things that attract
the convention guys.

Across the way, some of your friends
are taking battered old horns out of their cases.
A banjo's tuning up.
And somebody's fooling around with
an old upright piano.
Any minute now, they'll be bustin' loose
with a hand-me-down version of jazz.
Trying to hold onto the music
that all started somewhere around here . . .
somewhere, down around the river.
And you saw it all.

I guess you've seen about everything,
come to think of it.
Heard every sad story there is to tell,
and every bum joke.
Seen every stripper and every con man,
felt the bare feet of kids with long hair,
searching for something.
(God only knows what.)
You've heard the steady step of reformers
chasing sinners, drinking booze
from plastic cups.

That's your bag, old girl.
That's where you're at . . .
this is "New Orleens," as the tourists say,
and you're the star of the show.
Curtain's going up.
So, please to begin,
you lovable old phony.
You're not half as tough as you pretend.
I know.
I've seen you crying
when you thought no one was watching.